STEP FORWARD WITH

CURIOSITY

SHANNON WELBOURN
Crabtree Publishing Company
www.crabtreebooks.com

STEP FORWARD!

Author
Shannon Welbourn

Series research and development
Reagan Miller

Editorial director
Kathy Middleton

Editors
Reagan Miller, Janine Deschenes

Series Consultant
Larry Miller: BA (Sociology), BPE, MSc.Ed
Retired teacher, guidance counselor, and certified coach

Print and production coordinator
Katherine Berti

Design and photo research
Katherine Berti

Photographs
Dreamstime: © Hongqi Zhang (aka Michael Zhang), p 17
Shutterstock: © Anca Dumitrache, p 12; © mariakraynova,
 p 14 (bottom right); © Popova Valeriya, p 15 (bottom right)
Wikimedia: E2v, p 6 (center book);
 NASA, pp 8 (inset), 9 (right)
Other images by Shutterstock

Library and Archives Canada Cataloguing in Publication

Welbourn, Shannon, author
        Step forward with curiosity / Shannon Welbourn.

(Step forward!)
Includes index.
Issued in print and electronic formats.
ISBN 978-0-7787-2782-8 (hardback).--
ISBN 978-0-7787-2824-5 (paperback).--ISBN 978-1-4271-1829-5 (html)

    1. Curiosity--Juvenile literature. I. Title.

BF323.C8W45 2016   j153.8   C2016-903357-0
                                          C2016-903358-9

Library of Congress Cataloging-in-Publication Data

Names: Welbourn, Shannon, author.
Title: Step forward with curiosity /Shannon Welbourn.
Description: New York : Crabtree Publishing Company, [2017] |
 Series: Step forward! | Includes index.
Identifiers: LCCN 2016034716 (print) | LCCN 2016043366 (ebook) |
 ISBN 9780778727828 (reinforced library binding : alk. paper) |
 ISBN 9780778728245 (pbk. : alk. paper) |
 ISBN 9781427118295 (Electronic HTML)
Subjects: LCSH: Curiosity in children--Juvenile literature. |
 Curiosity--Juvenile literature.
Classification: LCC BF723.C8 M55 2017 (print) | LCC BF723.C8 (ebook) |
 DDC 155.2/32--dc23
LC record available at https://lccn.loc.gov/2016034716

Crabtree Publishing Company

www.crabtreebooks.com   1-800-387-7650

Printed in Canada/102016/IH20160811

Published in Canada
Crabtree Publishing
616 Welland Ave.
St. Catharines, Ontario
L2M 5V6

Published in the United States
Crabtree Publishing
PMB 59051
350 Fifth Avenue, 59th Floor
New York, New York 10118

Published in the United Kingdom
Crabtree Publishing
Maritime House
Basin Road North, Hove
BN41 1WR

Published in Australia
Crabtree Publishing
3 Charles Street
Coburg North
VIC 3058

CONTENTS

WHAT IS CURIOSITY?

Why is Earth called the Blue Planet? How do we know what dinosaurs looked like? When someone is curious, they ask questions to learn about things that interest them.

Curiosity is the **desire** to learn or know something. People who are curious are excited to **explore** and learn new things. They ask questions and work to find answers. What kind of things do you have questions about? Curiosity drives you to develop a deeper understanding about things that interest you.

Everyone has curiosity. Just like a muscle in your body, you need to use it to keep it strong.

When you ask questions, you start to explore new ideas. Each new question you ask helps you learn things you didn't know before. Answers can lead to new questions and ideas. Curiosity helps you develop an active mind, which means that you are constantly thinking and questioning.

Curiosity can lead you in new directions. These kids are curious about how trees grow. They are working together to explore answers!

WHY IS CURIOSITY IMPORTANT?

Curiosity is important because it opens your mind to learning about the world and discovering new things.

Curiosity has helped shape our world. Think about all of the amazing inventions around the world. These creations or discoveries would not have happened without curious minds. What would our world be like if Thomas Edison had not been not curious about **electric** light? Or what if Alexander Graham Bell and others had not been curious about communications through telephone lines?

When a curious person sees a problem to solve, they start asking questions. They look beyond what is already known and search to understand more. They look for possibilities to create or improve things. With curiosity, learning becomes an exciting journey of discovery!

*A curious mind came up with the idea to use robots in factories to make work easier. Curiosity can lead to **innovations**.*

CLARA MA

Following your curiosity leads you to topics and activities that interest you.

Name: Clara Ma

From: Prairie Village, Kansas

Accomplishment: Winner of the Mars Science Laboratory essay competition

Clara Ma was always fascinated with stars, planets, and space. Clara's grandma helped her curiosity grow by talking to her about **constellations** of stars in the night sky. Clara was also curious about what might exist in the universe beyond the stars. One day in science class, she learned about an essay competition to name the **Mars Rover**, a robot that was being sent to space to explore Mars. She thought of her own curiosity about space and felt the rover represented others' curiosity about space, too. Her essay suggested naming the rover "Curiosity." Her idea won!

Clara Ma was just 12 years old when she won the competition for naming the Mars Rover, "Curiosity."

"Curiosity is the passion that drives us through our everyday lives. We have become explorers and scientists with our need to ask questions and wonder."

—Clara Ma, from her winning essay

CURIOSITY AT HOME

Community

School   Home

Your home is the first place that your curiosity grows.

At a young age, you explore and learn new sights and sounds. As you get older, you can develop your curiosity by watching and learning from your family members. Curious people value what others can teach them.

Maybe your dad makes amazing cookies and you are curious to know how he does it.

You can build your curiosity by asking questions and learning about your family members. What was life like for them when they were your age? Your parents, grandparents, or caregivers all have their own interesting stories to tell. Ask questions! Pay attention and listen closely to the stories they share. You may discover that they were curious kids like you!

STEP FURTHER

Think of a question you could ask to learn something new about a family member.

Curious people know they can learn from others around them.

CURIOSITY AT SCHOOL

Community

School   Home

When your curiosity grows, you learn more. Let your interests drive you, and never stop on your path to learning!

While you are at school, you are constantly learning new things. People who are curious enjoy learning and exploring new ideas.

You can grow your curiosity by showing that you are excited to learn. Don't be afraid to ask questions when you don't understand. There is nothing wrong with saying you don't know the answer. Asking questions and finding answers builds curiosity.

STEP FURTHER

What is something you have been interested to learn more about? How can you explore the topic to learn more about it?

Curious people are active learners. They don't wait for someone to tell them answers. They take action to find out things for themselves. New learning often begins by asking "what," "why," "where," "when," "who," and "how." Finding answers to these questions gives us a basic understanding of something. To dig deeper, curious people ask questions such as, "What would happen if...?" and "How do we know...?"

If you were curious about how polar bears survive in the Arctic, you might ask questions such as, "What do polar bears eat?" and "What would happen if the Arctic got warmer?"

CURIOSITY IN YOUR COMMUNITY

Community

School

Home

A community is a group of people who live, work, and play in a place. Your home, school, and neighborhood are part of your community.

Being curious about how the world works is the first step in discovering ways to improve it. The world is a huge place—and we can begin by being curious in our communities.

sports event

aquarium

science center

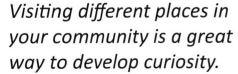

Visiting different places in your community is a great way to develop curiosity.

Curious people are open to new experiences. This means they are willing to learn and try new things. Sometimes you may not even know you are interested in something until you spend some time learning about it. Many libraries and community centers offer free clubs or classes for kids to join. Ask an adult to help you learn what programs are available in your community. From hiking on local nature trails to visiting a nearby farm, each new experience is a chance to discover and grow. You may be surprised by what you learn and develop a strong interest to explore more.

ROTARY CLUB EXCHANGE

Name: Rotary Club Exchange

From: Around the world

Accomplishment: Offers programs for youth to explore their curiosity by visiting new places.

Do you ever wonder how people live in other parts of the world? Curious people are often interested in people, places, and things beyond their own communities. This curiosity helps people better understand how we are all connected.

Some organizations have programs that give young people a chance to travel to other countries and learn about different ways of life. For example, the rotary club is a community group that offers a youth exchange program. The program provides young people a chance to live in another country for up to one year.

Different organizations around the world offer exchange programs. These exchange students are carrying their country's flags.

Students in the program live with host families and attend school. They learn about and experience a new **culture**, or way of life. Exchange students also teach others about their own culture and share what life is like where they live.

STEP FURTHER

Are you curious about a certain country or part of the world? What country would you want to visit if you took part in a youth exchange program?

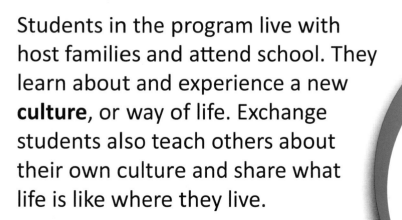

Some exchange students may learn a new language. This student is learning to read and write in Chinese.

OVERCOMING CHALLENGES

Challenges can get in the way of our curiosity. A challenge is something that is difficult to achieve, such as finding answers to difficult questions. Sometimes there are no easy answers to our questions, and it can be challenging to keep our curious minds going.

We wonder and develop many questions about the world around us. Sometimes our questions are easy to answer. Some may be more difficult to explore. It's okay to admit that you don't know something. When you do, you allow yourself to think of the next steps to come up with an answer, such as asking others for help or finding a new **resource** for information. The journey, or **process**, of learning and discovery matters more than finding the right answers. By being curious, you will keep learning and discovering new ideas throughout your life. Let your curiosity guide you on a journey of lifelong learning!

It can be a challenge to be curious about something that you can't explore in person, such as outer space. Overcome this challenge by finding other resources to learn from, such as books, the Internet, or other people.

ENCOURAGING CURIOSITY IN OTHERS

Each person's curiosity develops in different ways. Something you find interesting may not be of interest to someone else.

We cannot tell others what they should be curious about—but we can show others our excitement for learning new things. You can encourage others' curiosity by helping them explore their interests.

STEP FURTHER

What is something you are interested in and could share with others?

Curious people teach others and are open to learning from others, too.

When we are **enthusiastic** about a topic, our excitement may lead others to develop an interest. Sharing your love of learning could also encourage them to explore something they find interesting. You may also discover ways to **collaborate** with others. Each person may be curious about different things—but when you put their ideas together, everyone's mind grows.

Your curiosity about exploring outer space combined with your friend's interest in drawing comics could help you learn and create in new and exciting ways.

CURIOSITY IN ACTION!

"We keep moving forward, opening new doors, and trying new things, because we are curious and curiosity keeps leading us down new paths."

—Walt Disney, Animator and Business Owner

Take Action! You can learn more about topics that interest you by reading books, visiting websites, talking to people, going on fieldtrips, or trying out something for yourself.

*Remember: You can never know all there is to know about something!

Use the ideas and tips below to help you grow your curiosity!

Start a Question Journal: Create a notebook to record your questions. Try to write in it each night before you go to bed. Your questions could come from something that happened during the day, a new thing you noticed, or something you saw on television, or anything else. Write down your questions so that you can go back and explore them when you can.

Here are some journal question starters to get you started:

• What would happen if…?
• How can I solve the problem?
• What is the best way to….?
• How does it work?

LEARNING MORE

BOOKS

Hanson, Faye. *The Wonder*. Templar, 2015.

Kamkwamba, William & Mealer, Bryan. *The Boy Who Harnessed the Wind*. Dial Books, 2012.

Yamada, Kobi. *What Do You Do with an Idea?*. Compendium Inc., 2014.

WEBSITES

http://inspiremykids.com/2016/14303/
This link encourages curiosity with inspiring quotes, biographies, and project ideas.

http://wonderopolis.org/home
This site's content includes "wonder of the day," quizzes, informative articles, and hands-on activity suggestions.

http://mars.nasa.gov/msl
Mars Science Laboratory focusing on the Curiosity Rover.

WORDS TO KNOW

collaborate [k*uh*-LAB-*uh*-reyt] verb To work together with others

constellations [kon-stuh-LEY-shuhns] noun Groups of stars seen in patterns

culture [KUHL-cher] noun The shared beliefs and traditions in a place

desire [dih-ZAHY*UH* R] verb The longing for something that brings enjoyment, such as learning

electric [ih-LEK-trik] adjective Describing something powered by electricity

enthusiastic [en-thoo-zee-AS-tik] adjective Full of interest and excitement

explore [ik-SPLAWR] verb To investigate or learn about something

innovations [in-uh-VEY-shuhns] noun Something new or different that is introduced

Mars Rover [mahrz ROH-ver] noun A robotic machine sent by NASA in the United States to explore Mars

passion [PASH-uhn] noun A strong enthusiasm or desire

process [PROS-es] noun A set of steps or actions followed to achieve something

resource [REE-sawrs] noun Supplies or support, such as books, needed to do something

INDEX

ABOUT THE AUTHOR

Shannon Welbourn is a freelance author of educational K-12 books. She holds an honors BA in Child & Youth Studies, and is a certified teacher. Shannon works full-time as a Library and Media Specialist. In this position, she works closely with teachers and teacher candidates, helping to inspire and develop a passion for learning. Shannon lives close to Niagara Falls and enjoys vacationing in the Muskokas with her family.

24